Durable Goods

poems by

Gordon Johnston

Finishing Line Press
Georgetown, Kentucky

Durable Goods

Copyright © 2021 by Gordon Johnston
ISBN 978-1-64662-415-7 First Edition
All rights reserved under International and Pan-American Copyright Conventions. No part of this book may be reproduced in any manner whatsoever without written permission from the publisher, except in the case of brief quotations embodied in critical articles and reviews.

ACKNOWLEDGMENTS

The author thanks the editors of the following journals and anthologies where earlier versions of the poems in this collection first appeared:

Southern Poetry Review: "Durable Goods," "His Empty Oil Tin"

Writing on Napkins at the Sunshine Club: "Her Father's Pants"

Many Mountains Moving: "Tattoos"

Stone, River, Sky: An Anthology of Georgia Poets: "Canoe"

An earlier version of "The Morning After He Ran the River" appeared online on the Matthew's House Project website

Publisher: Leah Huete de Maines
Editor: Christen Kincaid
Cover Art: Whitney Ott
Author Photo: John Legg
Cover Design: Elizabeth Maines McCleavy

Printed in the USA on acid-free paper.
Order online: www.finishinglinepress.com
also available on amazon.com

Author inquiries and mail orders:
Finishing Line Press
P. O. Box 1626
Georgetown, Kentucky 40324
U. S. A.

Table of Contents

Durable Goods 1

Photograph, 1941 2

The Elements 3

Pasture Pond 4

Even the Dirt 5

His Pawpaw's Razor 6

Tattoos 7

Cassette Deck 8

Watching Jaws with Johnny 9

After Tom's Father Died 10

Her Father's Pants 11

Gathering Rocks and Stones 12

Bi- 13

Note at the Trailhead 14

Letter to Anya, Cirque of the Towers Trail, Wyoming 15

Letter to Anya, Dinwoody Glacier Trail, Wyoming 16

Letter to My Brother from Seven Islands Shoals 17

Cheat River: Packing the Pack 18

Canoe 20

My Grandfather's Empty Oil Can 21

Pockets 22

The Morning After He Ran the River 23

High Falls, Shavers Fork of the Cheat River 26

For Emma, Micah, and Graham

Durable Goods

Demand for them is down, the commentator says—a bad sign.
People can't afford the pressed metal boxes that cool their perishables
and cleanse their delicates. I wait for the number to call
to ask this question: why is desire not enough? For I have it
in spades for preservation, cleansing, agitation. A durable good
is so far past due, my one man's deprivation ought to give rise
to a region-wide recovery. The sail-less Maersk ships,
bigger than malls, ferrying their tonnage of containers,
should all be thrumming through the ocean to me and my house,
where need is so dire, so strong and centripetal that it must make
their compass needles read wrong, must draw them to a pitiful new pole—
a negation that the planet turns on. No number, though. It isn't a call-in show.
And why ask when you already know. Desire is not demand—that enormous
     we
that will have its wish whatever it costs. Desire accepts—expects—to be told
     No.
Can prosper on it. Deferred, desire grows. Demand refused explodes.

The problem is the keeping, not the having—good is always *going*.
Follow the needle tracks back until they vanish from the arm
of your junkie niece or brother, until you hold again a baby.
Or heft the hammer and square, the tools that framed the home
before this home. The hands that knew their use are gone.
The blackened skillet and cornbread mold, the topless churn,
a hand-smithed clevis—durable ghosts gather as you grow older,
as you keep on keeping these things that gone souls own. They hold
their forms. Goodness is a right grip struck on such tools—
a certainty, a seasoned grasp of what mortal needs each can fill, and how.

Fire, nail, muscle, mule, made to do their lasting work—the
hammer's rhythm, the plowing pace, the flue hum—
sacraments by which generations held their place in the world
and their world in its place, alive and in truck with mystery,
singing one part in a local, mortal harmony. This waiting is not better,
though it opens empty time in our lives for pictures and sugar,
boxes to talk and play and make music for us. The ships come on,
homing, full of their barren, stillborn Christmas.
They will until we demand a living that isn't death.

Photograph, 1941

My father's father, younger than I am,
    squats in his black suit, his arm around
my five-year-old father, whose own arm
    drapes over his dad's shoulder. Behind them,
the apple tree that persisted until I came,
    behind it the board fence of their big yard
that was the very small Johnston farm,
    where corn, tomatoes, potatoes, greens,
turnips, pecans, pears, and a milk cow prospered.

    The black and white photo seems too bright.
The decades have blurred their smiles and lightened
    edges in the print. The intensity of the morning
sun is not what makes the image sing. The boy and man
    cast a dark shadow leftward out of the frame.
In the background, the apple leaves shine
    against the deep shade around the trunk.
In the foreground, my grandfather's hand hangs down
    his lanky length—has been caught
just above its silhouette on the bare ground,

a dirt I know. The picture makes me feel found.
    My father's father's strong fingers—one set resting
on his only boy's thigh, the other open in the gesture
    of harvest, thumb slightly out, opposable, as if picking
a tomato or pole bean or pear—are in action, untouched
    by arthritis. My father's hands are for toys.
His face is my son's. His ears. The picture is a mirror
    I see into across seventy-two years,
a caught moment of the motion that made me,
    that made Micah and Graham in the image of us three.

    I rest in the shade of those two acres,
    the father who fed his family from them,
the father they grew. My own growth gathered itself there.
    Day by day, secondhand sun is taking back
its instant of light on apple leaves and these fathers, slowly,
    no pain. It can't take back the fruit, the grain,
        or the grip of the roots. It can't take back our name.

The Elements

Emma, three, sees a big balloon over a used car lot.
What makes it go up there, Daddy?
I answer *Helium. A gas.*
She nods: *We put gas in the car!*
Once again I can't say what I know,
can't tell her there is an absence with a name,
a nothing that gives rise to balloons. I try—
Like air. Like what a fan makes. Like when you breathe.
Does she know she breathes? It's hard to see right now,
I say, feeling like my own father. Did he believe
his own self? Once I heard a preacher
in Hog Hammock say the trinity was simple:
*You got your solid in God, who ain't changing,
your liquid in Jesus, filling that human shape
to bring you baptism, and you got the Holy Ghost,
unseen and brooding over you this minute—
all different forms of the same thing.*
I wish one of them would come and explain helium
to me and Emma both, but you know how it is:
they mostly stay way up there.

I plan future answers to her elemental questions:
*diamonds are water with backbone. Fire is whole summers
of sunlight unwinding from wood.* Are all fathers this flaky?
What air fills our heads? After Em came I found myself
pouring coffee slow to fit more into the mug.
Lord, give me cup enough to catch this pour.
May we realize that some vacancies rise.

Pasture Pond

    Come home, I look across my parents' yard through slack barbed wire
at the pasture pond where I fished every summer evening of my fourteenth year.
    The peepers fill the dusk as fully as this pool still brims its banks—same shape,
same shag of surrounding pines, though the willow at its shallow end is gone.
    Twenty years ago I last slipped through the fence to stand by the water
and cast a spinner in. I have eyes to see and ears to hear: it feels like enough,
    seeing the water across grass and over two fences and the road between them,
watching its pliant skin wrinkle with wind. It laps and invites, but this is still the
        country.
    Trespasses the boy me got by with might get the old man shot. Even here I'm
        there,
anyway, remembering the reel zing, the lure plop—to feel a bluegill seize a beetle
        spin
    and run, its muscle thrumming through the rod, was to be strung to an angry
        hunger
I thought I could land. I wasn't even a grown man before a stronger hunger
    set its hook in me. By this pond after my junior prom I watched the sun rise
in tails and jeans, the mist and the circles spreading on the surface as moist and
        momentary
    as the girl I had dropped off home at midnight, as possibly offering.
We had reached too far inside each other for me to still feel so alone. I solved the
        ache
    by skipping stones. For forty years I have been fifteen. I lift a red chip. I loft it,
sidearm, through the gloam. The water breaks. Breaks. It wobbles, then heals. Like
        home.

Even the Dirt

kept breathing a small breath, says Ted Roethke
in his bit about the root cellar. I carry that lungful
myself—the dirt more than the breath, the damp dust
ague of my grandmother's earth-walled room
of shelved preserves, the jars creepily lit by the one bulb,
crude oil jewels collecting their sift of grit from the floor above.
We've met, Ted, only in your poems and in your teaching
of my teacher's teachers, yet you can say how loam unmakes me—
how that rectangular, house-roofed grave grew me.

My father made soil. Bales of peat moss, foot-tubs of perlite,
vermiculite, and sweet yellow sand that I mixed with a hoe
for him to sprout seeds in. You should smell it wet, that Milky Way
of muck. A soaked flat glittered like a candle in a mica mine.
There's no counting the neighbors and strangers that ate what it grew,
the fruit it breathed out from burial, as dirt will always do.

His Pawpaw's Razor

Every dawn as I cut myself back with it, rinsing away a grit of pelt
to preserve my mask of boy, I have to shave slowly lest I nick my lip,

my cheek mole, the dells that edge my Adam's apple. The blade—
as long as my thumb, thin as a page of Galatians—drawn down my face

like a shade, makes a ripping gliss in the cranked-shut chrome jaws.
I angle the edge along the facets of my face, then up my overhang of chin,

where I must bear down a bit, my wrist wide awake to roughs and rises.
The least blade-snag will mean an hour of bleeding. I am both the field

and the mower, like my grandfather on his father's forty acres—tiller, seed-
sower, this farm the ground he grew from. I can see the geography of his jaw,

his hands easing an axe to the grindstone he let the boy-me turn. I hear the word
hone as I twist the razor's handle to free, rinse, and dry the blade. The stone,

white and pitted as old bone, rasped a silver bevel onto the blade. How I wanted
to own it—to keep and keen an edge, every day, was the secret to being grown.

Tattoos

God, to be a page, letters in my skin, not under it, sandy ink mingled and clotted with my blood into permanence, word made flesh in me, on me so that I'm a tombstone, a paint rock, a heart-carved tree slowly warping my lovers' names with my own growth. In the Haggadah, each letter of the alphabet begged God to let the world be wrought through her. *Bet* won. *Be*: saying it made all so. Words must be left as evidence, to ease the loneliness in places or to sharpen it, to needle in our passage through. Our bodies subway cars, bridges, boulders, great granite hills written, branded, worked with proof souls live there—souls needing not dead wood to write on but the first and last thing: this body. The print pierces just deep enough never to be shed, to ink my bleeding into *Mother*, runes, Jesus's face, a dragon in a spiral. Old wine in new skins. Notes for the final.

Cassette Deck

The wheels roll, reeling Neil Young from one pole
to the other, the brown ink of tape singing as un-cursively
as is conceivable over the heads in my Tacoma dash.
The deck tongues the slippage, magnetic taste buds
touching dust like Braile, wailing into my five-speed monk's cell
*Farmer John o-wee-oh o-wee-oh I'm in love with your daughter
o-wee-oh o-wee-oh Yeah the one o-wee-oh o-wee-oh
with the sham-pain eyes.* Under *the* Marshall-amped, over-
driven distortion, under the words, I hear the Pioneer breathing
as it reads—the frictive hiss as song is lifted, glissando
spooling of the familiar raw falsetto, the sustained, against-
the-grain Les Paul grind, the tape taut as a line hooked
into a diving tarpon, a-zing with brutal ecstasy. Held—
nailed—by it, here in my truck but dragged by its hook
toward a maw that has already, orgasmically, swallowed
me, I say *Yes* to being drawn between cranks in these
tight quarters, *yes* to the meeting that metes out this music,
to the contact that makes contact, the rub that wears down
the womp and stomp and wah-wah, that will play it to death.
How I feel this music unsealing my flat, plastic mortality,
unreeling me. *O-wee-oh o-wee-oh:* keeps me singing as I go.

Watching *Jaws* with Johnny

Bending River Trail, 1989

The boat is going down. The world is Roy Scheider and a rifle,
foundering, flotsam slopping as he takes aim, his glasses gone,
at the gaping maw that has eaten Shaw and Dreyfus,
that will eat him and then all else that its dead eye lands on.
Roy, the good sheriff, won't go easy. We love him, my girlfriend's
father and me, we see the man in him—the husband, the dad,
the drinking buddy, the law. He won't lose until he has lost.
He fires a slug into the snout. The shark plows on.
A second round skips past it. Roy throws the bolt back
with his fist, then forward with the heel of his hand,
drawing a bead, cursing what is coming hard to kill him,
talking back to whatever it is that has brought them both here,
to make him the fish food, the chum he knows he is to become,
to the universe that has made him and brought him before
this homing tank of cartilage. Too mad to feel fear,
barrel hand dead steady as a hammer, Roy waits. Waits.
He fires. When the fish explodes, something more than joy
jolts us from the couch. The shared pleasure in how completely
Roy's manhood has been measured—his kept head, his eye
for the O2 tank, his blade-sight savvy—holds us up
at least three heartbeats before we fall back to the couch,
shark sidemeat raining down around Roy and the wreck.
Satisfaction courses like a drug in our blood:
a weary smoker of a working man who should not have
has won. He can't swim and has beaten the sea. He is one.
It feels like a *we*, that *he*, and it will be, soon: Dreyfus
will surface, OK after all, and say *Quint*? It will come home
who is gone. For now, we are two men, one witness, with trigger
fingers, trouble, and women—two men, wide alive, kicking the sea.

After Tom's Father Died

Two weeks after the graveside, Tom brings to my front porch a box:
antique tins of split-shot sinkers, weedless hooks in clear zip bags
turning brittle, a Bomber Bushwhacker that has at least ten years on me,
on ambush in its ambered box.

If any one of these hits the water, he says, *that's better than throwing it away.*
We've paddled all of two rivers together, not fast, just too brisk for me to fish
(though on the Flint four years ago I landed three bass on five casts
when we beached to pee).

My dad wasn't much for fishing. The Bushwhacker eyes me with its ebony pupil,
barbs out, red along its back, gold-orange along its glittery flank. It's maw gapes
around the eyelet—pugnacious, bellicose. The lure poses less as prey than
provocation, its vintage ingenuity tooled and wise

to a largemouth's aggression. The bronze barbs brutal, the colors beautiful,
lifelike. Like life, which, the old folks used to say, *is a casting off.*
Because I was eleven and lived for June evenings hooking bluegill
from a farm ponds, I heard *Life is a casting out.*

As soon as possible, I'll tie the Bomber on a line and toss it into a tangle
of tree roots in the Ocmulgee's edge. I'll treasure it by risking its loss.
To feel it shudder through the current is a way to honor my friend's father.
Together we may land a lunker floating on that living water.

Her Father's Pants

She sneaks them to her room while he is sleeping,
careful not to trip on their long legs.
Heavy in her hands, their weight is half denim,
half what his pockets hold—things with uses
she doesn't know. Metal things, mostly—
a beaded chain of keys (the teeth on one
worn smooth), blades soot-gray as pencil leads
folded into bone, a double handful (for her)
of male faces, each with its own year, its own
trust in God. The belt's length if she unsnaked it
from the loops would be her height exactly.
When the buckle tinkles, that means midnight.
Three round mint candies are left of a roll.
She holds one on her tongue for breakfast,
letting it make her mouth cold. The wallet
she loves for its salted truckseat smell, for how
it flops open and there she is, waist-deep
in a tomato hole she is sure she remembers.
Dollars in that leather hinge wear down.
Get rubbed warm. She puts it back. She waits,
eager to hear him wake up and wonder where
his pants went. He will go to perk the coffee
and, secretly, she will lug the bucket of these dungarees
back, happy to carry every heavy thing that he does.

Gathering Rocks and Stones

The pocketing I do beside rivers goes back to my father,
who wanted big ones, half-loaves and eyeless potatoes
of stone taken from a blurring current. He owned
no shorts or bathing suit and every rock he raised
he rolled up pants legs for. His own white knee
was deep as he would go. Sight didn't guide him,
but his free, feeling feet, the curve of his arch
like a palm fitted itself to the clefts and curves
of the right heft of feldspar. Not one resisted him.
Each came up easily, wet and tame, at rest, translated
in air, their wait to slip back under, to gather again
a silt nest, already begun. They held still in his young
hands, as inert and alive and ancient as a sleeping child.
Not anything. Not nothing. Ballast, borrowed for a while.

Bi-

Bi- as in *-ped*, as in *-cycle*—is the phoneme for me
in motion, the twoness of my legs loping a trail

or the sidewalk to work, the twin-spin of spoked
wheels rolling me out and back home with enough speed

to make a breeze, even uphill. My Fuji has twice
the axels of the entire inhabited solar system,

oh so oiled that they carry me like a king.
Every circle can be surfed if you wedge in

where the curl begins. What this means
for my bicameral brain, for my two-room heart,

my matched lungs, kidneys, and cajones
I can't precisely say, except that these twins make me

improvise always—keep me keeping my balance
between two whirling wholes that halve me. Body

and soul. Father and gland. Opposing poles
divide my home against itself and make it stand.

Note at the Trailhead

> *Habituated bears have cut*
> *bear bag lines tied too low.*

Let this be a sign unto you, I go, as we walk
into the mountain's maw, slowed by heavy packs.
We're snacks carrying snacks. Good to know.
Grimey gives a little fake laugh: *Tie it high—*
so? A cub with a K-bar can still climb.
Do they chew the cord? Click out
one claw and saw through? We
drop the subject once we begin
to descend down into the noun
both our brains
are verbing:
gorge.

Letter to Anya, Cirque of the Towers Trail, Wyoming

Dear Anya,

You would like that the marshy meadow
our boots sank into as we looked for a camp
brought Emily's *boggy acre* rolling into my mouth.
Following the other two downslope from the trail
in the woods to an open dell, feet squelching
in the melt of spent blizzards just under the grass,
I felt my socks soak. To hold off my anger—wet boots
high up are no joke—I called myself *Boggy acher,*
my perfect name then and there, same rhythm
as *Bellyacher*, which from my father meant
Quit your bitching. That kick in the pants let me
be there, angling toward a copse of pines
along a stream fed by the subsurface water
on which we had just walked. So I was better
to the world that Em had written to me.
She never carped, I bet. We came to an outcrop
of rock under the grass, a slight, dry swell
of ground, just as the wind chilled us.
Happy and wordless, we dropped our packs. Home.
We pitched our gossamer tents in the gusts.
I zipped in. My hands too cold to write this—
zero at the bone—I dozed, rolled in down,
daffy with altitude, dreaming in syllables
and sounds, of your laughing at this,
postmarked from some tiny Wyoming town.

Letter to Anya, Dinwoody Glacier Trail, Wyoming

Dear Anya,

Four mornings before I found out in Crowheart,
as I followed two young men a hundred-mile walk
was making into friends down a disappearing trail
in the Wind River Range, a water ouzel tried to tell me.
Snowmelt thundered over rocks in the waterfall
I was last to cross. I was not ashamed to sit and shinny
along the fallen fir trunk, near bank to far, mist
cooling my face. The ouzel may have flown
from the rapid below—ouzels walk river-bottom rocks
in fast, frigid water to feed, then fly out dry, quick.
He may have shot under me, between the downed tree
and the seethe of creek, or over me. My eyes
were on my way forward, the silvered bare grain
of what passed for a bridge. The weight on my back
was winnowed to my body's basic needs, but still
the pack's heft could tip me and drop me in,
so I settled, eyes down, for his song as I palmed
and thigh-ed myself along. He lit upstream: I caught
from the corner of my vision a long-legged hunch
and flit: before my boot met the bank he had flown.
I wrote song. No—just his call: *zeet. Zeet. Zeet. Zeet.
Zeetzeezeet.* My semi-friends gone, I stood still,
listening, hearing and not hearing that I was alone.

Letter to My Brother from the Seven Islands Shoals

Running the river alone to get away, to wordlessly
        pray, I match the current blurring between boulders.
                It carries me and holds me in place. I have saddled
                        a snake that journeys through forms—that hisses
and chops through rocks, then, soundless, glisses
        'round a bend. Under me the muscle of dew, rain,
                second-hand sea, underground aquifer, ripples.
        If I could stay writ on this rolling liquid
I would be delivered like a letter to its delta
        that never wrote to me. Your poems carry me down
                each shoal, my boat's bow is blunt as your worn pencil
                        and busy as your bluetick's snout tracking 'coon.
Nosing through the rapids, I ride your gurney
        through the hospital hall. That glide is this one.
                Your pen trickled postcard poems from your chemo chair
that bear me along. Sent mail, like this boat's bottom,
        takes damage getting there. What that travels doesn't?
The Ocmulgee scars itself: sandbars sift downstream,
        soil sucks from under sycamores, island points strain
                planks, trash, and whole trees into drifts of accidental
architecture. This is to show you these isles, how they lean
        upstream, resisting the flow. Their trees' branches
                so nearly span the channel—so nearly fingertip the bank's
                        boughs—that they make the shade of a living cave,
        a corridor of breath, a green gullet as apt to cradle
as to swallow sticks, skiffs, whatever comes.
        The river can't help it. It has to go—snow to stone to
                stream, culvert to creekbed, journey between oceans
                        that weaves from well to well, breathed into
                            then out of thunderheads.
If in this long loop, this huge pouring zero feeding and breaking
        the mountains' bones, one of us slips under—so?
                Where either of us goes, the other will follow.

Cheat River: Packing the Pack

We gather together to ask the gorge's blessing:

                        armysocks in nylon shorts in old shirt in packtowel in wool sweater
                freeze-dried food book-flat in foil pouches and a can of beans
            two cups in two bowls in cook pot
      thin tent rolled tight
    sleeping bag

                              all nested in the pack, wound 'round by my therm-a-rest, as placental of my gear as it will be under me.

Next, zipped in baggies:

                    raincoat and cap
               (poems, coffee, creamer, wipes)
          (duct tape, compass, AAs, AAAs, headlamp, binocs)
      (notebook, spork, Bic, pen, cord, torch, patches, soap)

Side pocketed:

(Water)   (Water)

      See, Shaver's Fork of the Cheat, our thrift, our perfectly poor kit.
      In voluntary poverty we come to honor your excesses—your prodigal
        pissing away of current and scree, birch, fir, and teasel, your miles
      of sky left lying for any passing thieves. Spent sandstone and chert,
       blown vaults of turned and polished pebbles—we pack light
      to promise your shredding of feral tender will not be wasted on us.

Truck stuck by gully-rut in the logging road, we carry in what will carry us through
                          down mountain
                                              dis-

                                                                                                          solving

        trail
                              nettle-edged
                                                                                       boot
squelch in bog patch

                                                                        rockcrop tripspot
about drops Bill,
         then{though I go softshoe}me

                              until we lay our minimal all in the crisp flame of your
meadow grass
         to fish.

We give back the first green-black bass as soon as you grant her, writhing outrage
in lit   air.
Each one that hooks me is like a live wire grabbed: plunge of hunger, thrum of
muscle   fed.
The dead quicken in the packed feathers of the flesh that fights me, death the life in
you Cheat—current in you, each fish a current in the Shaver's current.
                                        Your bass who catch us we release
                                          hip-deep in your blurred unscrolling, lit
                                             wicks
                                                of cold. We throw ourselves back
                                            (not) standing still in the current (not)
                                             real

We two not two   Mountain and river (not) two   Shyster's drop our widow's mite
         offering

         Emptied, we come in gloam to what we packed in.
                  We unroll, see what we can live without. We lean into the lack.
         Bill cracks branches. I pitch the skin we will sleep in.
                  Smallmouth retell their stories.

                                             We let the fire lick our wounds.

    Two stars   Four

                  Our beans begin to bubble.

Canoe

She begins and ends, comes and goes, in confluence,
her bow and stern a merging of gunwhales, arrow ends of a boat-long
bending. To kneel within her is to be notched on the current's taut line.

She is less a weapon to cut water than a soft answer said to it—a *yes* spoken
to this sentence or that of the river's shifting sermon. Midship, like the water
that rolls her on, she widens, her bottom, like the riverbed's, an oxbow.

She is ordinal and original, quick and dead, ending as she began,
in the shape of a wave, a curl in air whose outer edge, followed,
becomes the rounded keel, trued to the river's wide will.

Filled by a falls, she would still float, limning the green skin of the water—
of the river, in her, yet still all herself, knowing as she is known—emptied of me.
Going on.

His Empty Oil Tin

Small, round, its screw-on spout slender as a steeple,
  the tip crooks like Adam's finger on the Sistine ceiling
(or like God's. He was as old as God, as able and original,
  better at sparing his tools from wear). Use has dimmed
and burnished the bronze finish. My hand wants to take it up,
  old vessel suited to its use, to fit its curve between my first
and second fingers and let my thumb love the springy, instant
  return of its pressed base, the tree frog chirp it makes:
the crick of tending. This spout-tip touched bead after bead
  to axels, gears, bearings. It kept a house of quiet hinges.
He taught it to my father, this male care—the worth
  of easing friction, the clean, greasy smell, the worn shine.
    The oiled, silent song of the work going on.

Pockets

When you get up, pull on empty ones:
Never wake to the same old freight.
Walk your rooms light and empty and load up
deliberately, deciding again about all you carried
yesterday—each key, the army knife, smooth stones.
Choose to bear each card and photo, your debts
and memberships and your children's faces, your license
to steer machines, your fold of legal tender.
To carry each all day on your person, their weight
should be worth it. Pockets are your preparedness,
so think which locks will need turning,
what silver your thirst might call for.
Read the scrap numbers, the dates on coupons.
Be reminded of bargains missed before. Know
that you could go out empty, wearing the room
to bring home the small new shines you find.

The Morning After He Ran the River

The morning after he ran the river,
the preacher's son wakes up forty-one,
not as young or sore as he expected, listens
to the coffee trickle. Yesterday a rock under
a wave stood his boat straight up and shot him
out of it. Bruised, he sat on a wet boulder, sodden,
boatless, believing he was stranded until he turned
and saw like a blurred blue splinter his kayak under
the river's moving skin, ten yards downstream. He waded
two steps, stumbled, barely caught the keel toggle as he swept
past her. He had to pull hard to stand, against the water's strong will.
His thighs plowed furrows standing still. He strained against the rock
and flow wedging her under: not a quiver. Chin-deep, he reached blind
inside the capsized cockpit. His groping fingers found his Big Gulp cup. Ah.

Gulp by Gulp, he bailed the boat. It was an anti-communion,
a de-immersion that rejected the greater will, the provenient grace
of the river's gradient. His 'yak unburied from baptism would rise again
to its old life, be bourne again on the tension between deeps and sky, rest
on the promises of the element that frothed to subsume it, the river ever
born and ending, schist and water, drink, drowner, earth-drill, doldrum.
He dipped and dipped. He dipped. He dipped until his mind died, until
what he did was him, until he was big and little dipper and all dippers
in between, until he entered unto infinitive: to dip.
And the stones of his shoulder were ground to powder. And he dipped.
And the cold of the current entered even his eyes. And he dipped.
And from afar, from under the bed of the current came one word,
ur-syllable heard in his right ear, under the water. Again he dipped:
again it sounded. His free hand, holding on, felt plastic flex.
He conceived of the nothing that he was building in the boat:
the zero of a vacuum, growing negation, space emptied
of water and air, so pure with absence each cupful
puckered the sunk, bottom-up boat. This is
the zero that utters the single warped word,
the voice of no breath, the absence
under air, sun, river, shoal—all.
He was sowing void..

To get home, he had to meet and puncture the vacuum: had to put breath
back in the boat. How he needed a hose—! He plunged the cup
bottom up through the river and into the cockpit, sending Gulp

after Gulp of air into the drowned hull until the stern seemed
to stir in its sleep, then to rise almost to the surface. His body,
weary, thrilled: he bounced on the balls of his feet, slipped
grabbing at the kayak as the current knocked him down.
His foot found a cleft rock, pushed him back up again.
The cup became the grail then—lost, gone
from his numb fingers. He stared down-
stream so long he saw four red-ears,
each its own home, poke a head up
for air.

His lungs were the last cup he had. He breathed deep to dive
and blow, burning with cold, gripping the edge of the boat.
Eyes shut, against the rush of river he pulled his face
between rock and cockpit, blew his whole breath
in an unseen stream of silver bubbles inside,
where he heard them burst and fizz, where
their air levered the kayak up the single
inch it took to free her and to sweep
her tail left so that she held him
under against the bottom cobble.
The tussle wasn't long. His mind
had just oxygen enough to see that his own
breath would kill him, to picture his absence:
his good truck, orphaned at the put-in, his house,
unkempt, so still it felt haunted even to him, his body
pressed here forever, a four-petal flower under the river's
warped pane for redeye, shoal bass, and alligator gar to witness.

> He must have been a fulcrum.
> He can't see how else he floated free.
> The current piled up, he guesses, watching
> the coffee drip, it pushed against the bobbing stern
> until it pried the bow out of the cleft that had held it.
> This would explain his three blue ribs and the lack of water in his lungs
> when he woke, face against gravel, on the left side of the hole he still thought
> had killed him, his boat bumping a rock behind him and also—he gradually
> came to feel—butting the backs of his thighs like a dog that wants to be walked.
> The 'yak-nudge confirmed he was no ghost. He lay there grounded
> against the sweet gravel, blessed, freezing. He swallowed

the small flake of mica that was in his mouth. He was left
over. He had voided a little into the slosh of shallows.
A long while later he stood and stepped to the stern,
the boat both sunk and afloat, suspended just below
the surface. Her nose growled into the pebbles
as he shouldered the keel up, water cascading
from the cockpit in a clear spill like a tributary
spring. It is this moment he remembers,
going on forty-one, and going on,
waiting to pour the first bone
china cup: how easy
the emptying was.

High Falls, Shaver's Fork of the Cheat River, Late June

Because we have backpacked from Bemis
between the gleam of the tracks, boots on gravel
all the way, I'm done in by every suppleness I witness:
current rounding over a river-wide warp of stone,
drift sticks licked gray and skinless by the pour
until they're vascular and tenderized, vulnerable
as the inside of a girl's wrist, the rhododendron thicket's
springs and bends and green slap fight of passage that musks
me up with semi-stiff rubbings. Branches bow, neither
low nor high, but always—always—mid-thigh.
                                        Still, I pass
upstream, descend again down the moss boing of bank
to the clear bustle of a deep hole below a shoal.
The surface is a warble of cold through which brook trout,
fearless, see me magnified, their fins fingering the cobbled bottom.
God, the give and resistance of this old, broken whole, the flow—
the easy hold of each fish in the Cheat's ceaseless blow. I'll fool not
one, but the river has me, too—rod, soul, mind. So I throw and throw
and throw.
            Daylight runs out. The bright rails and black ties, wave
and laurel and brook and hole—they all go. Mountain and river roll into
a single shadow, still not speaking, in words I ought to know.

Gordon Johnton's stories, poems, and essays have appeared in *American Fiction, The Georgia Review, Fourth Genre, Southern Poetry Review,* and other magazines and in several anthologies (among them *Stone, River Sky: An Anthology of Georgia Poems* from Negative Capability Press, 2015; *The Southern Poetry Anthology* from Texas Review Press, 2013; *Writing on Napkins at the Sunshine Club* from Mercer University Press, 2013). Perkolator Press published Johnston's letter-press chapbook *Gravity's Light Grip* in 2008. Johnston also collaborates with potter Roger Jamison on clay pages—poems and very short stories Johnston writes in clay that Jamison then wood-fires into stoneware tiles in a cave kiln in Juliette, Georgia. These clay pages have been featured in three gallery shows. Johnston earned a PhD in American literature from the University if Georgia in 1995 and has taught creative writing and contemporary literature at Mercer University since 1996. As Writer in Residence at Ocmulgee National Monument for three years, he canoed all of the Altamaha, Ocmulgee, and Oconee rivers and co-authored with historian Matthew Jennings *Ocmulgee National Monument: A Brief History with Field Notes* (Mercer University Press, 2017); Johnston's portion of the guide is a naturalist's notebook of creative nonfiction about the national historical park in Macon, Georgia, which contains eight Mississippian mounds in a wild setting.

www.ingramcontent.com/pod-product-compliance
Lightning Source LLC
LaVergne TN
LVHW041516070426
835507LV00012B/1601